baking •home

Chef
express

Published by:
TRIDENT REFERENCE PUBLISHING
801 12th Avenue South, Suite 400
Naples, Fl 34102 USA

Tel: + 1 (239) 649-7077
www.tridentreference.com
email: sales@tridentreference.com

Home Baking
© TRIDENT REFERENCE PUBLISHING

Publisher
Simon St. John Bailey

Editor-in-chief
Susan Knightley

Prepress
Precision Prep & Press

Includes Index
ISBN 1582796564
UPC 6 15269 96564 1

Printed in The United States

introduction

Making bread, cake and pastry is the ultimate
pleasure of the home cook. Nothing compares
to the delicious smell of hot muffins, spicy
cookies, perfect croissants or olive bread.
There's something magical about these home
baked specialties related to the bliss of
kneading the dough and a feeling of awe at
the surprising transformations a
warm oven can perform.

home baking
introduction

Flour and yeast

Whether using regular or whole grain wheat flour, by itself or combined with cornmeal or oatmeal, making the perfect yeast bread requires the rising time is respected. Too little rising will cause coarse bread crusts and a gummy texture.

Dough will always require more flour than the recipe states, since every kneading is done on a lightly floured surface.

Beating

A cake fails to be moist and airy when the butter and sugar mixture was not properly beaten and creamed or because eggs were added too quickly. Make sure to use a spoon to fold in the flour gently, without stirring, so as not to eliminate the air incorporated to the mixture through beating

The oven

In baking bread as well as pasty and cakes, the temperature of the oven is essential. Ovens too high cause thick, heavy crusts on breads. With cakes and pasty, the surface may overburn while the center undercooks. For the best results, always follow recipe instructions carefully.

When is it done?

- A cake is done when a wookedn stick inserted in the center comes out clean, without batter adherence.
- In the case of bread, just hit lightly on the bottom: if it souds hollow, it's done.

How to preserve the dough

Fresh yeast dough stores perfectly well, plastic-wrapped in the refrigerator. To use, let stand at room temperature and knead again, with some flour, before baking. Once baked, the loafs can also be frozen, hermetically sealed.

Difficulty Scale

■□□I Easy to do

■■□I Requires attention

■■■I Requires experience

yeast
based dough

■■□ | Cooking time: according to use - Preparation time: 2 hours

ingredients

> **1 teaspoon active dry yeast**
> **pinch sugar**
> **2/3 cup/170 ml/5 1/2 fl oz warm water**
> **2 cups/250 ml/8 oz flour**
> **1/2 teaspoon salt**
> **1/4 cup/60 ml/2 fl oz olive oil**

method

1. Place yeast, sugar and water in a large bowl (a) and mix to dissolve. Set aside in a warm, draught-free place for 5 minutes or until foamy (b).

2. Place flour and salt in a food processor and pulse once or twice to sift. With machine running, slowly pour in oil and yeast mixture and process to form a rough dough. Turn dough onto a lightly floured surface and knead for 5 minutes or until soft and shiny (c). Add more flour if necessary.

3. Lightly oil a large bowl, then roll dough around in it to cover the surface with oil. Cover bowl tightly with plastic food wrap and place in a warm, draught-free place for 1 1/2-2 hours or until dough has doubled in volume. Knock down and remove dough from bowl. Knead briefly before using as desired. Bake at 200°C/400°F/Gas 6.

Makes 250 g/8 oz dough

tip from the chef

Don't knead the dough longer than the recipes recommnend because it will become too elastic and lose tenderness while cooking. However, it is necessary to do so to deaerate it, but then it must be left to rise until it doubles its size.

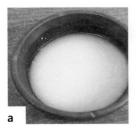

a

b

c

baking powder
based dough

■ ■ □ | Cooking time: according to use - Preparation time: 20 minutes

method

1. Sift flour and baking powder together into a bowl, add sugar. Using your fingertips, rub in butter until mixture resembles fine breadcrumbs.
2. Make a well in the center of flour mixture and using a round-ended knife, mix in egg and enough milk to form a soft dough.
3. Turn dough onto a lightly floured surface and knead with fingertips until smooth. Using heel of hand, press dough out evenly, shape as desired, then bake at 220°C/425°F/Gas 7 until cooked and golden.

Makes 500 g/1 lb dough

ingredients

> **2 cups/250 g/8 oz self-raising flour**
> **1 teaspoon baking powder**
> **2 teaspoons sugar**
> **60 g/2 oz butter, chopped**
> **1 egg, lightly beaten**
> **1/2 cup/125 ml/4 fl oz milk**

tip from the chef
This is a good alternative to using a yeast based dough when time is short. Cooking time will usually be a little less when using a baking powder based dough.

soda bread

■□□ | Cooking time: 40 minutes - Preparation time: 30 minutes

method

1. Sift together flour, bicarbonate of soda and salt into a mixing bowl. Rub in butter using fingertips until mixture resembles coarse breadcrumbs. Make a well in the center of the flour mixture and pour in milk. Using a round-ended knife, mix to form a soft dough.

2. Turn dough onto a floured surface and knead lightly until smooth. Shape into an 18 cm/7 in round and place on a greased and floured baking tray. Score dough into eighths using a sharp knife. Dust lightly with flour and bake at 200°C/400°F/Gas 6 for 35-40 minutes or until loaf sounds hollow when tapped on the base.

....
Serves 8

ingredients

> **500 g/1 lb flour**
> **1 teaspoon bicarbonate of soda**
> **1 teaspoon salt**
> **45 g/1¹/₂ oz butter**
> **500 ml/16 fl oz buttermilk or milk**

tip from the chef

A loaf to make when you need bread unexpectedly. Wonderful spread with lashings of treacle or golden syrup. Soda bread is made with bicarbonate of soda rather than yeast so it requires no rising. It is best eaten slightly warm.

simple
cornbread

■□□ | Cooking time: 25 minutes - Preparation time: 15 minutes

ingredients

> **125 g/4 oz sifted plain flour**
> **4 teaspoons baking powder**
> **³/4 teaspoon salt**
> **30 g/1 oz sugar**
> **125 g/4 oz polenta**
> **2 eggs**
> **1 cup/250 ml/8 oz milk**
> **30 g/1 oz butter**
> **butter, to serve**

method

1. Sift flour with baking powder and salt. Stir in sugar and polenta. Add eggs, milk and melted butter. Beat until just smooth.
2. Pour into a 23 x 23 x 5 cm/9 x 9 x 2 in tin lined with baking paper and bake at 220°C/440°F/Gas 7 for 20-25 minutes.
3. Remove from tin and cut into squares to serve with butter.

....

Serves 4

tip from the chef

Polenta can be replaced by fine rolled oats. This recipe is ideal for an afternoon tea.

unleavened
bread

■ ■ □ | Cooking time: 4 minutes - Preparation time: 45 minutes

method

1. Combine flour and salt in a bowl and make a well in the center. Add water and clarified butter and mix to a smooth dough. Rest dough for 20 minutes.
2. Take 2 tablespoons of dough and roll into balls. Roll each ball to make very thin oval shapes. Place breads on a nonstick baking tray and bake at 220°C/425°F/Gas 7 for 2-4 minutes or until lightly golden.

ingredients

> **4 cups/500 g/1 lb flour**
> **1 teaspoon salt**
> **1 cup/250 ml/8 fl oz water**
> **45 g/1¹/₂ oz clarified butter, melted**

....
Makes 12 rounds

tip from the chef

To clarify butter, put it in a small saucepan, bring to the boil and cool. Remove the top residue and the serum deposited at the bottom; use the central layer, which is the clarified butter.

thyme and chili cornbread

■□□ | Cooking time: 45 minutes - Preparation time: 15 minutes

ingredients

> **1 cup/155g/5 oz wholemeal flour**
> **³/4 cup/125 g/4 oz polenta**
> **3 teaspoons baking powder**
> **60 g/2 oz grated Parmesan cheese**
> **2 tablespoons chopped fresh thyme**
> **1 teaspoon finely grated lemon rind**
> **¹/2 teaspoon chili flakes**
> **155 ml/5 fl oz milk**
> **¹/4 cup/60 ml/2 fl oz olive oil**
> **2 eggs, lightly beaten**
> **3 sprigs fresh thyme**

method

1. Sift flour, polenta and baking powder together into a bowl. Return husks to bowl. Add Parmesan cheese, thyme, lemon rind and chili flakes and mix to combine.
2. Place milk, oil and eggs in a small bowl and whisk to combine. Stir milk mixture into dry ingredients and mix well.
3. Spoon mixture into a lightly greased 11 x 21 cm/4¹/2 x 8¹/2 in loaf tin. Smooth surface of batter with a knife, decorate with thyme sprigs and bake at 190°C/375°F/Gas 5 for 45 minutes or until loaf is cooked when tested with a skewer. Stand loaf in tin for 5 minutes before turning onto a wire rack to cool slightly. Serve warm.

Makes an 11 x 21 cm/4¹/2 x 8¹/2 in loaf

tip from the chef

Lemon thyme is a delicious alternative to ordinary thyme in this recipe. If using lemon thyme, omit the lemon rind.

cheesy herb bread

■□□ I Cooking time: 45 minutes - Preparation time: 15 minutes

method

1. Place flour, baking powder, salt, stock powder, rosemary, dill, chives, sage and 12 g/4 oz cheese in a bowl and mix to combine.

2. Combine egg, milk and butter. Add egg mixture to dry ingredients and mix to combine.

3. Spoon mixture into a greased and lined 11 x 21 cm/4¹/₂ x 8¹/₂ in loaf tin, sprinkle with remaining cheese and bake at 190°C/375°F/Gas 5 for 45 minutes or until cooked when tested with a skewer. Turn onto a wire rack to cool.

Makes one 11 x 21 cm/4¹/₂ x 8¹/₂ in loaf

ingredients

> **2 cups/250 g/8 oz all purpose flour, sifted**
> **2 teaspoons baking powder**
> **1 teaspoon salt**
> **1 teaspoon chicken stock powder**
> **2 tablespoons chopped fresh rosemary or 1 teaspoon dried rosemary**
> **2 tablespoons chopped fresh dill**
> **2 tablespoons snipped fresh chives**
> **2 tablespoons chopped fresh sage or 1 teaspoon dried sage**
> **185 g/6 oz grated tasty (mature Cheddar) cheese**
> **1 egg, lightly beaten**
> **155 ml/5 fl oz milk**
> **30 g/1 oz butter, melted**

tip from the chef

Another time, try combining the flavors of thyme, bay leaves and fennel seeds with the rosemary and sage for a loaf infused with the classic "herbes de Provence".

olive
soda bread

■□□ I Cooking time: 45 minutes - Preparation time: 15 minutes

method

1. Place butter, sugar and egg in a food processor and process until smooth. Add wholemeal flour, flour, bicarbonate of soda, baking powder and milk and process to form a soft dough.

2. Turn dough onto a lightly floured surface and knead in olives. Shape dough into a 20 cm/8 in round and place on a lightly greased and floured baking tray. Using a sharp knife, cut a cross in the top. Sprinkle with fennel seeds and salt and bake at 200°C/400°F/Gas 5 for 45 minutes or until cooked.

Makes one 20 cm/8 in round loaf

ingredients

> **125 g/4 oz butter, softened**
> **¼ cup/60 g/2 oz sugar**
> **1 egg**
> **3 cups/470 g/15 oz wholemeal flour**
> **3 teaspoons baking powder**
> **1½ cups/185 g/6 oz flour**
> **1½ teaspoons bicarbonate of soda**
> **1½ cups/375 ml/ 12 fl oz buttermilk or milk**
> **125 g/4 oz black olives, chopped**
> **2 teaspoons fennel seeds**
> **1 teaspoon coarse sea salt**

tip from the chef

The famous Irish soda bread is influenced here by the Mediterranean flavors of fennel and olives. You may use one of the many types of marinated olives available, if you wish.

cheese
and bacon damper

a

■□□ | Cooking time: 30 minutes - Preparation time: 20 minutes

method

1. Rub the margarine into the flour and baking powder (a) until mixture resembles coarse breadcrumbs.
2. Stir in parsley, chives, cheese and bacon (b). Mix well.
3. Combine the egg and milk, stir into the dry ingredients (c) and mix to a soft dough.
4. Turn dough onto a lightly floured board and knead lightly.
5. Shape into a cob, cut a deep cross in the center of the cob (d) and place on a sheet of baking paper on an oven tray.
6. Bake at 200°C/400°F/Gas 6 for 30 minutes or until hollow-sounding when tapped underneath.
7. Serve hot with a crock of butter on a buffet table, cut into small pieces.

....
Serves 6-8

ingredients

> 3 tablespoons margarine or butter
> 2¹/2 cups all purpose flour
> 3 teaspoons baking powder
> 2 teaspoons parsley flakes
> 1 teaspoon chopped chives
> 1 cup/125 g/4 oz grated tasty (mature Cheddar) cheese
> 2 rashers cooked bacon, finely chopped
> 1 egg
> ³/4 cup/180 ml/6 fl oz milk

tip from the chef

This bread is delicious when sliced thinly and served, just toasted, with a green salad and poached eggs.

b

c

d

mexican
cornbread

■■□ | Cooking time: 60 minutes - Preparation time: 35 minutes

ingredients

> **2 cups/350 g/11 oz polenta**
> **2 cups/250 g/8 oz all purpose flour, sifted**
> **2¹/2 teaspoons baking powder**
> **125 g/4 oz grated tasty (mature Cheddar) cheese**
> **60 g/2 oz grated Parmesan cheese**
> **12 pitted black olives, sliced**
> **12 sun-dried tomatoes, chopped**
> **100 g/3¹/2 oz canned sweet corn kernels, drained**
> **3 bottled green peppers, chopped finely**
> **2 eggs, lightly beaten**
> **1 cup/250 ml/8 fl oz milk**
> **³/4 cup/155 g/5 oz yogurt**
> **¹/4 cup/60 ml/2 fl oz vegetable oil**

method

1. Place polenta, all purpose flour and baking powder in a bowl. Add tasty (mature Cheddar) cheese, Parmesan cheese, olives, sun-dried tomatoes, sweet corn and green peppers in a bowl and mix to combine.

2. Combine eggs, milk, yogurt and oil. Add egg mixture to dry ingredients and mix until just combined.

3. Pour mixture into a greased 20 cm/8 in springform pan and bake at 180°C/350°F/Gas 4 for 1 hour or until bread is cooked when tested with a skewer. Serve warm or cold.

Makes one 20 cm/8 in round loaf

tip from the chef

Split wedges of this loaf and layer with savory fillings to create attractive sandwiches. This cornbread is also delicious served warm and topped with baked ricotta cheese.

spinach,
olive and onion bread

■ ■ □ I Cooking time: 25 minutes - Preparation time: 45 minutes

method

1. Prepare dough as described in recipe.
2. To make filling, heat olive oil in a large frying pan and cook onion until soft. Add garlic and sultanas and cook 1 minute longer. Add spinach and olives and cook over a medium heat until spinach just begins to wilt. Remove from heat and mix in mozzarella. Season to taste with black pepper. Set aside.
3. Knock down dough and knead lightly. Divide dough into four portions, and roll each out into 5 mm/¼ in thick circles. Place two circles on lightly oiled baking trays, then spread with filling to within 2.5 cm/1 in of edge. Cover with remaining circles and pinch sides together to seal edges.
4. Brush top with olive oil. Cover with a clean tea-towel and set aside to rise in a warm place until doubled in size.
5. Brush top with egg white and bake at 200°C/400°F/Gas 6 for 25 minutes, or until golden brown and well risen.

ingredients

> 1 recipe yeast based dough (page 6)
> 1 tablespoon olive oil
> 1 egg white, lightly beaten

filling

> 2 tablespoons olive oil
> 1 large red onion, sliced
> 1 clove garlic, crushed
> 1 tablespoon sultanas
> 750 g/1½ lb spinach, stalks removed and leaves shredded
> 125 g/4 oz stuffed green olives, sliced
> 3 tablespoons fresh mozzarella cheese, grated
> freshly ground black pepper

....
Serves 8

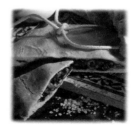

tip from the chef

A filled bread, almost a pie, this flat loaf makes a delicious snack or supper dish.

honey
oat loaf

■□□ | Cooking time: 45 minutes - Preparation time: 10 minutes

ingredients

> 1/2 cup/60 g/2 oz flour
> 1 cup/125 g/4 oz self-raising flour
> 1 teaspoon salt
> 1 1/2 teaspoons baking powder
> 1 cup/90 g/3 oz rolled oats
> 45 g/1 1/2 oz butter, melted
> 2 eggs, lightly beaten
> 1/4 cup/60 ml/2 fl oz water
> 1/2 cup/170 g/ 5 1/2 oz honey, warmed

method

1. Sift together flour and self-raising flour, salt and baking powder into a large mixing bowl. Stir in rolled oats.
2. Combine butter, eggs, water and honey and mix into flour mixture until just combined. Pour into a greased and lined 11 x 21 cm/4 1/2 x 8 1/2 in loaf tin and bake at 180°C/350°F/Gas 4 for 40-45 minutes or until cooked when tested with a skewer. Stand in tin for 5 minutes before turning onto a wire rack to cool completely.

Makes an 11 x 21 cm/ 4 1/2 x 8 1/2 in loaf

tip from the chef

Plain, or spread with a little butter and jam, this loaf tastes delicious. Honey can be substituted by grape syrup or molasses, and rolled oats by rice crispies or corn flakes.

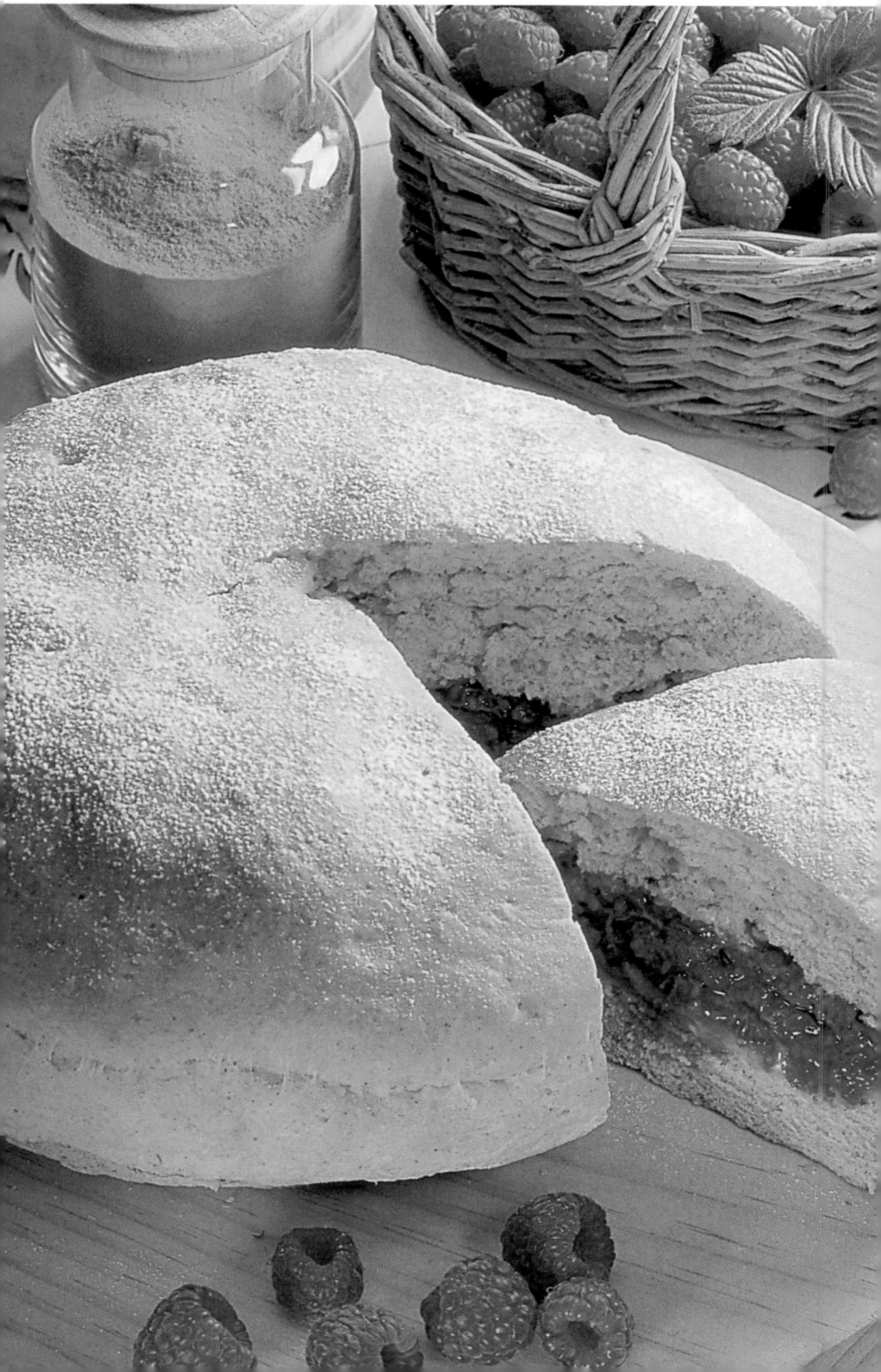

easy berry bread

■■□ | Cooking time: 35 minutes - Preparation time: 25 minutes

method

1. Sift flour, mixed spice and baking powder together into a bowl. Add sugar then, using your fingertips, rub in butter until mixture resembles coarse breadcrumbs.
2. Make a well in the center of flour mixture then, using a round-ended knife, mix in water and milk (a) and mix to form a soft dough.
3. Turn dough onto a floured surface and knead lightly until smooth. Divide dough into two portions and flatten each into an 18 cm/7 in round.
4. Sprinkle raspberries and sugar (b) over surface of one round leaving 2.5 cm/1 in around edge. Brush edge with a little milk and place remaining round on top (c). Seal edges securely using fingertips.
5. Place on a greased and lightly floured baking tray. Brush surface of loaf with a little milk and bake at 220°C/425°F/Gas 7 for 10 minutes. Reduce oven temperature to 180°C/350°F/Gas 4 and bake for 20-25 minutes longer or until cooked.

Makes one 18 cm/7 in round

ingredients

> 3 cups/375 g/12 oz all purpose flour
> 1 1/2 teaspoons ground mixed spice
> 4 teaspoons baking powder
> 1 1/2 tablespoons sugar
> 30 g/1 oz butter
> 2/3 cup/170 ml/5 1/2 fl oz water
> 1/2 cup/125 ml/4 fl oz milk
> 200 g/6 1/2 oz raspberries
> 1 tablespoon caster sugar
> 4 teaspoons milk, for brushing

tip from the chef

Butter absorbs odors easily, so keep it in the refrigerator covered and away from foods such as onions and fish or you will have a strong-smelling butter that will affect baked goods.

a

b

c

classic
blueberry muffins

■□□ | Cooking time: 30 minutes - Preparation time: 15 minutes

method

1. Sift flour and baking powder together into a bowl, add sugar and mix to combine.
2. Combine eggs, milk and butter. Add egg mixture and blueberries to dry ingredients and mix until just combined.
3. Spoon mixture into six greased 1 cup/ 250 ml/8 fl oz capacity muffin tins. Sprinkle with coffee sugar crystals and bake at 200°C/400°F/Gas 6 for 20-30 minutes or until muffins are cooked when tested with a skewer. Turn onto wire racks to cool.

ingredients

> 2¹/2 cups/315 g/10 oz all purpose flour
> 3 teaspoons baking powder
> ¹/2 cup/90 g/3 oz sugar
> 2 eggs, lightly beaten
> 1 cup/250 ml/8 fl oz buttermilk or milk
> 60 g/2 oz butter, melted
> 125 g/4 oz blueberries
> 2 tablespoons coffee sugar crystals

Makes 6

tip from the chef

Finely shredded orange peel can be added to this mixture to enhance the flavor of the blueberries.

Coffee sugar crystals are coarse golden brown sugar grains. If unavailable, raw (muscovado) or demerara sugar can be used instead.

apricot
oat bran muffins

■☐☐ I Cooking time: 20 minutes - Preparation time: 15 minutes

ingredients

> **2 cups/250 g/8 oz all purpose flour**
> **2 teaspoons baking powder**
> **1 cup/45 g/1¹/2 oz oat bran**
> **60 g/2 oz dried apricots, chopped**
> **60 g/2 oz sultanas**
> **1 egg, lightly beaten**
> **1¹/2 cups/325 ml/12 fl oz buttermilk or milk**
> **¹/4 cup/60 ml/2 fl oz golden syrup**
> **90 g/3 oz butter, melted**

method

1. Sift flour and baking powder together into a bowl. Add oat bran, apricots and sultanas (a), mix to combine and set aside.
2. Combine egg, milk, golden syrup (b) and butter.
3. Add milk mixture to dry ingredients and mix (c) until just combined. Spoon mixture into six greased 1 cup/250 ml/8 fl oz capacity muffin tins and bake at 180°C/350°F/ Gas 4 for 15-20 minutes or until muffins are cooked when tested with a skewer. Serve hot, warm or cold.

Makes 6

tip from the chef

Serve this muffin for breakfast or brunch fresh and warm from the oven, split and buttered and perhaps with a drizzle of honey.

a

b

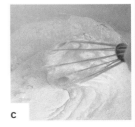

c

ginger pear cakes

■ ■ □ | Cooking time: 40 minutes - Preparation time: 35 minutes

method

1. Place sugar, oil, egg and vanilla essence in a bowl and beat to combine. Sift together flour, bicarbonate of soda, ginger and nutmeg. Mix flour mixture into egg mixture, then fold in pears and chopped ginger.

2. Spoon batter into six lightly greased large muffin tins and bake at 180°C/350°F/Gas 4 for 20 minutes. Reduce oven temperature to 160°C/325°F/Gas 3 and bake for 15-20 minutes longer, or until cakes are cooked when tested with a skewer.

3. To make ginger cream, place cream, sour cream and honey in a bowl and beat until soft peaks form. Add brandy and ground ginger and beat to combine. Fold in chopped ginger. Serve cakes hot or warm accompanied by ginger cream.

....

Serves 6

ingredients

- > 1/2 cup/125 g/4 oz raw sugar
- > 1/4 cup/60 ml/2 fl oz vegetable oil
- > 1 egg, lightly beaten
- > 1 teaspoon vanilla essence
- > 1 cup/125 g/4 oz flour
- > 1 teaspoon bicarbonate of soda
- > 1/2 teaspoon ground ginger
- > 1/2 teaspoon ground nutmeg
- > 2 pears, cored, peeled and finely diced
- > 155 g/5 oz glacé ginger or stem ginger in syrup, chopped

ginger cream

- > 1 cup/250 ml/8 fl oz cream (double)
- > 1/4 cup/60 g/2 oz sour cream
- > 1 tablespoon honey
- > 1 tablespoon brandy
- > 1/4 teaspoon ground ginger
- > 1 tablespoon finely chopped glacé ginger or stem ginger in syrup

tip from the chef

To make ginger in syrup, mix stem ginger with 6 tablespoons sugar and 1 cup water and reduce over low heat. To glaze ginger, cook it slowly in a frying pan with butter and sugar.

banana
choc-chip muffins

■□□ | Cooking time: 20 minutes - Preparation time: 5 minutes

method

1. In a mixing bowl, mash the banana, add the milk, egg and melted margarine (a). Mix well.
2. Stir the sifted flour, baking powder, sugar and choc bits (b) into the banana mixture, mix only until the ingredients are combined.
3. Spoon mixture into well-greased muffin tins (c). Bake at 190°C/370°F/Gas 5 for 20 minutes. Serve warm or cold.

....

Makes 12

ingredients

> 1 large ripe banana
> 1 cup/250 ml/8 fl oz milk
> 1 egg
> 1/4 cup/60 ml/2 fl oz margarine, melted
> 1 1/2 cups/185 g/6 oz all purpose flour
> 1 1/2 teaspoons baking powder
> 1/2 cup/120 g/4 oz caster sugar
> 3/4 cup/120 g/4 oz choc bits

tip from the chef

Muffins are ready when a skewer is inserted in the middle and it comes out clean and dry; remove muffins from tin and cool on wire rack.

a

b

c

herb rolls

■ ■ □ I Cooking time: 40 minutes - Preparation time: 35 minutes

ingredients

> **90 g/3 oz butter**
> **8 spring onions, finely chopped**
> **315 g/10 oz flour**
> **125 g/4 oz self-raising flour**
> **3 teaspoons baking powder**
> **1/2 teaspoon bicarbonate of soda**
> **4 teaspoons sugar**
> **1 tablespoon finely chopped fresh parsley**
> **1 tablespoon finely chopped fresh basil**
> **125 ml/4 fl oz buttermilk or milk**
> **3 eggs, lightly beaten**
> **1 egg, beaten with 1/2 teaspoon olive oil**

method

1. Melt butter in a frying pan and cook spring onions over a medium heat for 2-3 minutes or until onions are soft. Remove from heat and set aside.

2. Sift together flour and self-raising flour, baking powder and bicarbonate of soda into a large mixing bowl. Stir in sugar, parsley and basil. Combine milk, eggs and onion mixture and mix into flour mixture to form a firm dough.

3. Turn onto a floured surface and knead lightly until smooth. Divide dough into twelve portions and roll each into a ball, then place on greased and floured baking trays. Brush each roll with egg and oil mixture and bake at 180°C/350°F/Gas 4 for 30-35 minutes or until cooked through.

....
Makes 12 rolls

tip from the chef

Spring onions and herbs have been added to this soda bread recipe. The dough is then formed into rolls to make the quickest herb flavored rolls ever.

mushroom
muffins

■■□ I Cooking time: 25 minutes - Preparation time: 35 minutes

method

1. Sift flour and baking powder into a large bowl. Mix in mushrooms, rice, cheese and herbs.
2. Make a well in the center of the dry ingredients. Add the remaining ingredients. Mix until just combined (see note).
3. Spoon mixture into greased muffin tins until three quarters full. Bake at 200°C/400°F/Gas 6 for 25 minutes. Remove from tin. Cool on a wire rack. Serve hot or cold.

....
Makes about 12

ingredients

> **2 cups/250 g/8 oz all purpose flour**
> **1 tablespoon baking powder**
> **60 g/2 oz fresh mushrooms, chopped**
> **1/2 cup/75 g/2 1/2 oz cooked brown rice**
> **1/2 cup/60 g/2 oz shredded tasty (mature Cheddar) cheese**
> **1 tablespoon parsley flakes**
> **2 teaspoons chives, chopped**
> **125 g/4 oz margarine, melted**
> **1 cup/250 ml/8 oz milk**
> **1 egg, beaten**

tip from the chef

Don't worry if not all the flour is incorporated as this gives muffins their characteristic texture. Sixteen strokes is usually enough when mixing.

brandy
grape flan

■ ■ ■ | Cooking time: 20 minutes - Preparation time: 45 minutes

ingredients

> **155 g/5 oz prepared shortcrust pastry**

grape filling

> **250 g/8 oz cream cheese**
> **2 tablespoons bottled lemon butter**
> **1 tablespoon icing sugar**
> **500 g/1 lb large green grapes**

apricot glaze

> **3 tablespoons apricot jam**
> **1 1/2 tablespoons water**
> **2 teaspoons brandy**

method

1. Line a lightly greased 20 cm/8 in flan tin with pastry (a). Line pastry case with nonstick baking paper, weigh down with uncooked rice and bake at 200°C/400°F/Gas 6 for 10 minutes. Remove rice and paper. Reduce temperature to 180°C/350°F/Gas 4 and bake 15-20 minutes longer or until pastry is lightly browned. Set aside to cool.

2. To make filling, place cream cheese in a bowl and beat until soft. Mix in lemon butter and icing sugar. Spread cream cheese mixture over the base of pastry case.

3. Wash grapes and separate from stems. Cut in half and remove seeds. Arrange grapes in a decorative pattern (b) over cream cheese mixture.

4. To make glaze, heat apricot jam and water in a saucepan, stirring until jam melts. Push through a sieve. Stir in brandy and cool slightly. Brush glaze over grapes (c) and chill flan until ready to serve.

....
Serves 8

tip from the chef

Grapes can be replaced by plums or thin slices of mango.

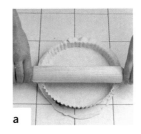

a

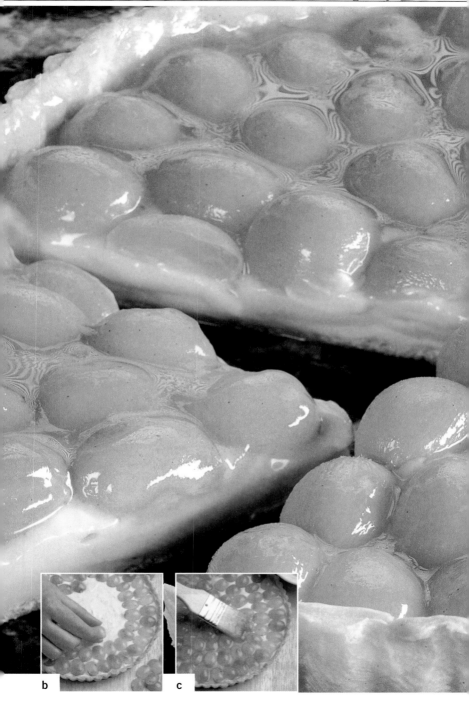

b

c

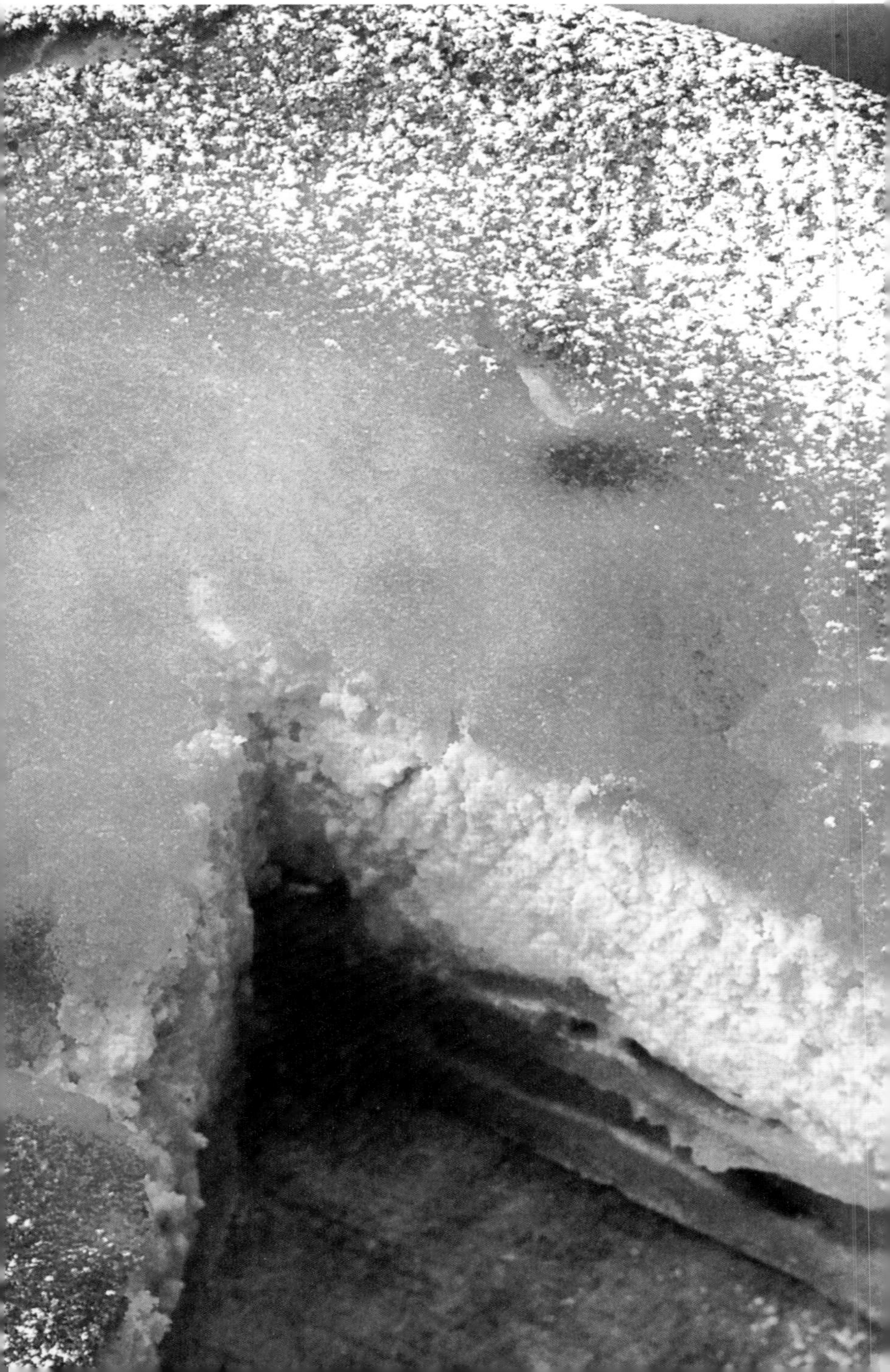

baked
apple cheesecake

■■□ I Cooking time: 90 minutes - Preparation time: 45 minutes

method

1. Roll out pastry to 3 mm/¹/₈ in thick and use to line a deep 23 cm/9 in flan tin with a removable base. Prick base and sides of pastry with a fork, line with nonstick baking paper and fill with uncooked rice. Bake at 190°C/375°F/Gas 5 for 10 minutes, then remove rice and paper and bake for 5-8 minutes longer or until lightly browned.

2. Melt butter in a frying pan, add apple slices and cook over a medium heat, stirring occasionally, until golden. Set aside to cool. Arrange apples evenly over base of pastry case.

3. To make filling, place all filling ingredients in a food processor and process until smooth.

4. Place egg whites in a separate bowl and beat until stiff peaks form. Fold egg white mixture into ricotta mixture. Carefully pour filling over apples.

5. Reduce oven temperature to 180°C/350°F/Gas 4 and bake for 1¹/₄ hours or until firm. Set aside to cool, then refrigerate overnight.

ingredients

> **200 g/6¹/₂ oz prepared shortcrust pastry**
> **30 g/1 oz butter**
> **2 apples, cored, peeled and sliced**

ricotta filling

> **750 g/1¹/₂ lb ricotta cheese**
> **4 eggs, separated**
> **¹/₂ cup/170 g/5¹/₂ oz honey**
> **1 tablespoon finely grated orange rind**
> **3 tablespoons orange juice**

············
Serves 8

tip from the chef

The secret of this cheesecake lies in whipping the egg whites very carefully. Once beaten they must be folded into the ricotta cheese mixture.

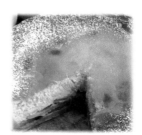

pear and walnut
upside-down pudding

■■□ | Cooking time: 80 minutes - Preparation time: 30 minutes

ingredients

> **3 tablespoons demerara sugar**
> **2 x 440 g/14 oz canned pear halves, drained and 250 ml/8 fl oz syrup reserved**
> **8 red glacé cherries, halved**
> **250 g/8 oz butter, softened**
> **4 eggs**
> **250 g/8 oz self-raising flour**
> **220 g/7 oz caster sugar**
> **125 g/4 oz chopped walnuts**
> **3 tablespoons maple syrup**

method

1. Sprinkle base of a greased and lined, deep 23 cm/9 in round cake tin with demerara sugar. Arrange pears (a) and cherries over base.
2. Place butter, eggs, flour and caster sugar in food processor and process until smooth. Stir in walnuts. Carefully spoon batter (b) over pears and cherries in tin and bake at 180°C/350°F/Gas 4 for 1-1¼ hours, or until cooked when tested with a skewer.
3. Place maple syrup and reserved pear juice in a small saucepan and cook over a medium heat until syrup is reduced by half.
4. Turn pudding onto a serving plate and pour syrup over. Serve hot or warm with cream or ice cream if desired.

....
Serves 8

tip from the chef
If maple syrup is unavailable, grape syrup, honey or molasses can be used.

a

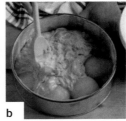

b

spicy apple cake

■□□ | Cooking time: 35 minutes - Preparation time: 10 minutes

method

1. Combine oil and sugar in a large bowl. Whisk in eggs and vanilla. Combine flour and spice in one bowl and apples, lemon rind and sultanas in another. Fold flour mixture and apple mixture alternately into beaten egg mixture.

2. Spoon mixture into a greased and lined 20 cm/8 in square ring pan and bake at 180°C/350°F/Gas 4 for 30-35 minutes or until cooked. Stand 5 minutes before turning out on a wire rack to cool.

Serves 12

ingredients

> 3 tablespoons oil
> 3/4 cup/190 g/6 oz caster sugar
> 2 eggs, lightly beaten
> 1 teaspoon vanilla essence
> 1 cup/125 g/4 oz self-raising flour, sifted
> 1 1/2 teaspoons ground mixed spice
> 410 g/13 oz canned unsweetened sliced apples, drained
> 1 teaspoon grated lemon rind
> 1/2 cup/80 g/3 oz sultanas

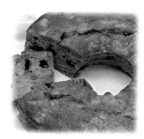

tip from the chef

A nice aroma for this recipe is obtained with a mixture of ground cinnamon, cardamom and allspice.

thumbprint
cookies

■ ■ □ I Cooking time: 12 minutes - Preparation time: 25 minutes

ingredients

> **185 g/6 oz butter, softened**
> **1/2 cup/45 g/11/2 oz icing sugar, sifted**
> **1 teaspoon vanilla essence**
> **1 teaspoon baking powder**
> **11/2 cup/185 g/6 oz all purpose flour**
> **1/2 cup/60 g/2 oz custard powder**
> **1/4 cup/60 ml/2 fl oz milk**
> **jam, lemon curd or chopped chocolate**

method

1. Place butter, icing sugar and vanilla essence in a bowl and beat until light and fluffy. Sift together flour, baking powder and custard powder. Fold flour mixture and milk, alternately, into butter mixture.

2. Roll tablespoons of mixture into balls and place on greased baking trays. Make a thumbprint in the center of each cookie.

3. Fill thumbprint hole with a teaspoon of jam, lemon curd or chocolate. Bake at 190°C/375°F/Gas 5 for 12 minutes or until cookies are golden. Transfer to wire racks to cool.

. . . .
Makes 30

tip from the chef

Wrap the dough in plastic food wrap and chill at least 30 minutes to make it easier to shape into balls. For a subtle toasty nut flavor, roll the balls in sesame seeds before making the thumbprint and filling.

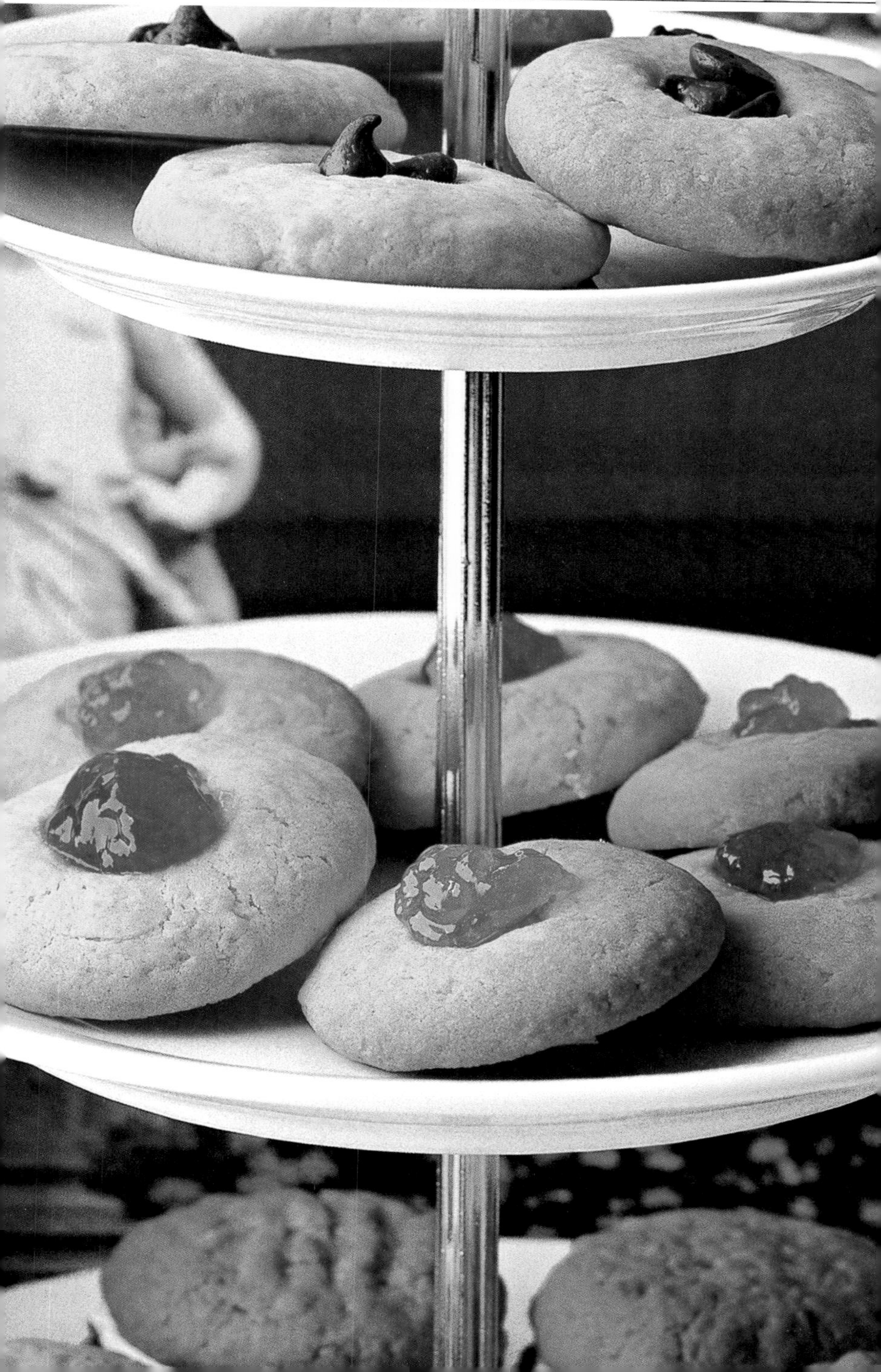

cinnamon
crisps

■■□ I Cooking time: 8 minutes - Preparation time: 25 minutes

method

1. Place butter and ³/4 cup/170 g/5¹/2 oz sugar in a bowl and beat until light and fluffy. Add egg and beat well.
2. Sift together flour, baking powder and bicarbonate of soda and stir into butter mixture. Turn dough onto a floured surface and knead briefly. Wrap in plastic food wrap and refrigerate for 30 minutes or until firm.
3. Place cinnamon and remaining sugar in a small bowl and mix to combine. Roll dough into small balls, then roll balls in sugar mixture. Place 5 cm/2 in apart on lightly greased baking trays and bake at 180°C/350°F/Gas 4 for 8 minutes or until golden. Remove to wire racks to cool.

....
Makes 25

ingredients

> **125 g/4 oz butter**
> **1 cup/220 g/7 oz caster sugar**
> **1 egg**
> **1¹/2 cups/185 g/6 oz flour**
> **¹/2 teaspoon baking powder**
> **¹/2 teaspoon bicarbonate of soda**
> **2 teaspoons ground cinnamon**

tip from the chef

Fat or shortening in whatever form makes a baked product tender and helps to improve its keeping quality. In most baked goods, top-quality margarine and butter are interchangeable.

triple
choc-chip cookies

■□□ | Cooking time: 15 minutes - Preparation time: 15 minutes

ingredients

> ¹/2 cup/120 g/4 oz caster sugar
> ¹/2 cup/75 g/2¹/2 oz brown sugar
> 175 g/6 oz margarine
> ¹/2 teaspoon vanilla essence
> 1 egg
> 1³/4 cup/210 g/7 oz plain flour
> 1¹/2 teaspoons baking powder
> ¹/2 cup/75 g/2¹/2 oz each choc bits, milk bits and white bits

method

1. Cream together sugars, margarine and vanilla essence. Add the egg and beat in well.
2. Sift the flour and baking powder together and add to the creamed mixture. Stir in the choc bits, milk bits and white bits.
3. Place teaspoonfuls of mixture onto lightly greased oven trays.
4. Bake at 180°C/350°F/Gas 4 for 15 minutes. Cool on tray 5 minutes before removing to wire tray to cool. Store in airtight container.

Makes 36

tip from the chef

Watch baking time carefully, as cookies cook quickly and can get burnt.

gingerbread
people

■■☐ | Cooking time: 10 minutes - Preparation time: 40 minutes

method

1. Cream together the margarine and brown sugar, and beat in the egg yolk, mixing well. Sift in the flour, bicarbonate of soda and ginger and gradually blend into the creamed mixture, along with the golden syrup. Knead lightly to make a soft dough.
2. Divide the dough into small portions. Roll out each portion of dough to a thickness of 1/2 cm/1/4 in between two sheets of greaseproof paper. Cut into shapes using cutters.
3. Place on lightly greased oven trays. Bake at 180°C/350°F/Gas 4 for 10 minutes. Cool on trays. Decorate with icing, if desired.

ingredients

> **125 g/4 oz margarine**
> **1/2 cup/75 g/2 1/2 oz brown sugar**
> **1 egg yolk**
> **2 1/2 cups/300 g/10 oz plain flour**
> **1 teaspoon bicarbonate of soda**
> **3 teaspoons ground ginger**
> **2 1/2 tablespoons golden syrup**

Makes approximately 20 shapes (depending on size)

tip from the chef

These charming cookie people are delightful for children. Tied with ribbons and hung on windows or Christmas trees, they are great decorations.

chili
soup biscuits

■ ■ □ | Cooking time: 18 minutes - Preparation time: 30 minutes

ingredients

> **2 rashers bacon, finely chopped**
> **250 g/8 oz flour**
> **3 teaspoons baking powder**
> **1/2 teaspoon salt**
> **90 g/3 oz butter**
> **90 g/3 oz grated mature Cheddar**
> **2 small fresh red chilies, seeded and finely chopped**
> **170 ml/51/2 fl oz milk**
> **30 g/1 oz butter, melted**

method

1. Cook bacon in a nonstick frying pan over a medium high heat for 3-4 minutes or until crisp. Remove from pan and drain on absorbent kitchen paper.

2. Sift together flour, baking powder and salt into a mixing bowl. Rub in butter with fingertips until mixture resembles coarse breadcrumbs.

3. Stir bacon, cheese and chilies into flour mixture. Add milk and mix to form a soft dough. Turn onto a floured surface and knead lightly with fingertips until smooth.

4. Using heel of hand, gently press dough out to 1 cm/1/2 in thick. Cut out rounds using a 5 cm/2 in pastry cutter. Place on a greased baking tray and brush with melted butter. Bake at 220°C/425°F/Gas 7 for 12-15 minutes or until golden brown. Remove from tray and cool on a wire rack, or serve warm spread with butter.

....
Makes 16 biscuits

tip from the chef

These biscuits are perfect to serve as appetizers with drinks on the rocks, like Pisco Sour or Frozen Margarita. They can be stored for quite some time in airtight containers.

croissants

a

b

c

■ ■ ■ | Cooking time: 25 minutes - Preparation time: several hours

method

1. Sift flour onto a board and divide into four. Take one quarter and make a well in the center. Place the yeast in this (a) and mix with about 2-3 tablespoons warm milk-and-water mixture. The yeast must be dissolved and the dough soft.

2. Have ready a saucepan of warm water and drop the ball of yeast dough into this and set aside. Add the salt to the rest of the flour, make a well in the center, add half the butter, softened (b), and work up, adding enough of the milk-and-water mixture to make a firm paste.

3. Beat on the board for about 5 minutes. Lift the yeast dough from the water –it should be spongy and well risen– mix into the paste thoroughly.

4. Turn into a floured bowl (c), cover with a plate and place in the refrigerator for 12 hours. Roll out the paste to a square, place the rest of the butter, cold, in the center and fold up like a parcel.

5. Give the paste three turns as for puff pastry, and a fourth if the butter is not completely absorbed. Rest the paste between every two turns and chill before shaping. When ready for shaping, roll out very thinly to an oblong shape, divide into two lengthwise and cut each strip into triangles. Roll up each one starting from the base and seal tip with beaten egg. Curl to form a crescent, then set on a dampened baking tray. Let stand for about 10 minutes then brush with beaten egg. Bake at 200°C/400°F/Gas 6 for about 25 minutes.

....

Serves 4

ingredients

> **375 g/12 oz flour**
> **15 g/¹/2 oz yeast**
> **¹/2 teaspoon salt**
> **150 ml/5 oz warm milk and water (half and half)**
> **185 g/6 oz butter**

tip from the chef
Croissant dough requires many stages of kneading and rising. The cooling time in the refrigerator can be replaced by 30 minutes in the freezer. The dough must then be kneaded again.

index